Summary

Lawmakers could increase federal revenues and encourage reductions in emissions of carbon dioxide (CO_2) by establishing a carbon tax, which would either tax those emissions directly or tax fuels that release CO_2 when they are burned (fossil fuels, such as coal, oil, and natural gas). Emissions of CO_2 and other greenhouse gases accumulate in the atmosphere and contribute to climate change—a long-term and potentially very costly global problem.

The effects of a carbon tax on the U.S. economy would depend on how the revenues from the tax were used. Options include using the revenues to reduce budget deficits, to decrease existing marginal tax rates (the rates on an additional dollar of income), or to offset the costs that a carbon tax would impose on certain groups of people. This study examines how a carbon tax, combined with those alternative uses of the revenues, might affect the economy and the environment.

How Much Revenue Could a Carbon Tax Raise?

Neither the Congressional Budget Office (CBO) nor the staff of the Joint Committee on Taxation has published an estimate of how much revenue a carbon tax might produce. However, CBO has extensively analyzed policies, known as cap-and-trade programs, that would similarly set a price on CO_2 emissions. Those analyses suggest that a carbon tax that covered the bulk of CO_2 emissions or the carbon content of most fossil fuel consumed in the United States could generate a substantial amount of revenue. For example, in 2011, CBO estimated that a cap-and-trade program that would have set a price of $20 in 2012 to emit a ton of CO_2 (and increased that price by 5.6 percent each year thereafter) would raise a total of nearly $1.2 trillion during its first decade.[1] In addition, total U.S. emissions of CO_2 would be about 8 percent lower over that period than they would be without the policy, CBO estimated.

How Would a Carbon Tax Directly Affect the Economy?

By raising the cost of using fossil fuels, a carbon tax would tend to increase the cost of producing goods and services—especially things, such as electricity or transportation, that involve relatively large amounts of CO_2 emissions. Those cost increases would provide an incentive for companies to manufacture their products in ways that resulted in fewer CO_2 emissions. Higher production costs would also lead to higher prices for emission-intensive goods and services, which would encourage households to use less of them and more of other goods and services.

Without accounting for how the revenues from a carbon tax would be used, such a tax would have a negative effect on the economy. The higher prices it caused would diminish the purchasing power of people's earnings, effectively reducing their real (inflation-adjusted) wages. Lower real wages would have the net effect of reducing the amount that people worked, thus decreasing the overall supply of labor. Investment would also decline, further reducing the economy's total output.

The costs of a carbon tax would not be evenly distributed among U.S. households. For example, the additional costs from higher prices would consume a greater share of income for low-income households than for higher-income households, because low-income households generally spend a larger percentage of their income on emission-intensive goods. Similarly, workers and investors in emission-intensive industries, who would see the largest decrease in demand for their products, would be likely to bear relatively large burdens as the economy adjusted to the tax. Finally, areas of the country where electricity is produced from coal—the most emission-intensive fossil fuel per unit of energy generated—would tend to experience larger increases in electricity prices than other areas would.

How Would Various Uses of the Revenues From a Carbon Tax Alter Its Economic Effects?

Lawmakers' choices about how to use the revenues from a carbon tax would help determine the tax's ultimate impact on the economy. Some uses of those revenues could substantially offset the total economic costs resulting from the tax itself, whereas other uses would not.

Using the Revenues to Reduce Deficits Would Decrease the Tax's Total Costs to the Economy.

At least part of the negative economic effect of a carbon tax would be offset if the tax revenues were used for deficit reduction. Federal budget deficits tend to result in lower

---

1. See Congressional Budget Office, *Reducing the Deficit: Spending and Revenue Options* (March 2011), pp. 205–206, www.cbo.gov/publication/22043. That revenue estimate accounts for the fact that the policy would have the effect of reducing income tax collections.

economic output over the long run than would otherwise be the case, by crowding out private-sector investment. Thus, policies that reduce deficits generally have a positive effect on the economy in the long run (although they can have a negative effect in the short term when the economy is weak).

Using the Revenues to Cut Marginal Tax Rates Would Also Decrease Total Costs. Lawmakers could also offset some of the negative economic effects of a carbon tax by using the revenues to reduce the existing marginal rates of income or payroll taxes—a policy known as a tax swap. Existing taxes on individual and corporate income decrease people's incentives to work and invest by lowering the after-tax returns they receive from those activities. Consequently, reducing those marginal tax rates would have positive effects on the economy.

Using the Revenues to Reduce Adverse Effects on Selected Groups Would Not Decrease Total Costs. Targeting revenues toward people who would be likely to bear a disproportionate burden under a carbon tax would provide them with relief, but such a policy would tend not to reduce the total economic costs of the tax. Thus, lawmakers would face a trade-off between the goals of helping those households most hurt by the tax and helping the economy in general. Lawmakers could use the revenues in more than one way to try to balance those goals.

How Would a Carbon Tax Affect the Environment?

Climate change resulting from an increase in average temperatures is a long-term problem with global causes and consequences, including effects on humans and ecosystems. Significantly limiting the extent of future warming would require a concerted effort by countries that are major emitters of greenhouse gases. Nonetheless, U.S. efforts to decrease emissions would produce incremental benefits, in the form of incremental reductions in the expected damage from climate change.

Researchers have attempted to estimate the monetary value of the future damage from climate change associated with an increase in CO_2 emissions in a given year—and thus the value of the benefits from a commensurate reduction in emissions—a measure referred to as the social cost of carbon (SCC). An interagency working group of the federal government estimated the SCC associated with a 1-ton reduction in CO_2 emissions in 2010 at about $21 (in 2007 dollars). Estimates of the SCC are highly uncertain, and researchers have produced a wide range of values. Those values are highest when researchers attach significant weight to long-term outcomes and when they incorporate a small probability that damage from climate change could increase sharply in the future—causing very large, or even catastrophic, losses. Delaying efforts to reduce emissions increases the risk of such losses. Given the inherent uncertainty of predicting the effects of climate change, and the possibility that it could trigger catastrophic effects, lawmakers might view a carbon tax as a reflection of society's willingness to pay to reduce the risk of potentially very expensive damage in the future.

The Revenue Implications of Taxing Carbon Dioxide Emissions or Fossil Fuels

Interest has been growing internationally and in the United States in taxing the carbon that is released into the atmosphere in the form of carbon dioxide when fossil fuels are burned. Advocates of a carbon tax in the United States cite two potential benefits from such a tax: It could serve as an important source of federal revenues, and it would reduce CO_2 emissions by setting a price on carbon dioxide—the most prevalent of the greenhouse gases that trap heat in the Earth's atmosphere. Such a price would ensure that the costs of products and activities that involve CO_2 emissions incorporate some of the potential costs of damage from climate change.

The amount of revenues that a U.S. carbon tax might raise would depend on the rate of the tax, how broadly it was applied, and the extent to which it led to declines in CO_2 emissions. Those revenues could be significant. For example, CBO estimated in 2011 that setting a price of $20 per metric ton on greenhouse gas emissions in the United States in 2012 and raising that price at a nominal rate of 5.6 percent per year would yield a total of $1.2 trillion in revenues over the 2012–2021 period.[2] Nearly 96 percent of that amount—or an average of $115 billion a year during that period— would come from the charge levied on CO_2 emissions (with the rest coming from the charge on emissions of other greenhouse gases). Such revenues would be roughly equivalent to the total amount that the U.S. government collects each year from excise taxes (including taxes on gasoline, tobacco, and alcohol) and would be much greater than annual receipts from estate and gift taxes or customs duties.

That $20 emission charge would reduce total U.S. emissions of CO_2 between 2012 and 2021 by about 8 percent, CBO estimated.[3] Because rising tax rates would lead to a decline in emissions, the amount of revenues generated by a carbon tax would eventually decline as well (the effect on emissions during the 2012–2021 period is incorporated in the revenue estimate above). However, if the tax rate grew slowly, it could produce rising revenues for many decades and allow the economy to adjust gradually to less-emission-intensive ways of producing goods and services.

The particulars of that 2011 analysis (including the initial price that companies would pay to emit a ton of greenhouse gases and the rate at which the price would increase) stemmed from the illustrative policy that CBO was analyzing; the policy was not meant to represent the price on emissions that would best balance the costs and benefits of

---

2. Congressional Budget Office, *Reducing the Deficit: Spending and Revenue Options* (March 2011), pp. 205–206, www.cbo.gov/publication/22043. That revenue estimate accounts for the effect that setting a price on emissions would have in reducing profits and wages (as discussed later in this report), thus lowering the revenues collected from income taxes.

3. That particular policy did not cover all CO_2 emissions (for example, it excluded emissions from small electricity generators). The policy would reduce covered CO_2 emissions over the 2012–2021 period by 10 percent, CBO estimated.

reducing emissions. The policy that CBO analyzed involved a cap-and-trade program similar to legislation that the House of Representatives passed in 2009. Under that policy, firms would pay the federal government for rights (or allowances) to emit greenhouse gases and could trade those allowances in a secondary market. In such a system, the price of allowances and the rate at which that price increased would depend on firms' actions.[4]

Some Key Issues in Administering a Carbon Tax

Carbon becomes part of the U.S. economy when coal, oil, and natural gas are extracted or imported. It enters the atmosphere, in the form of carbon dioxide, when those fossil fuels are burned. Analysts have tried to determine the point in that process at which it would be most cost-effective to levy a carbon tax. The tax could apply either to the carbon content of each fuel or to the CO_2 emissions released when the fuel is burned. (A ton of CO_2 contains 0.27 tons of carbon, so a price of $20 per ton on CO_2 emissions, as in the previous example, would be equivalent to a price of $73 per ton on the carbon content of fossil fuels.)

In addition to deciding where to apply the tax, designers of a carbon tax would need to consider what entities or uses of fossil fuels, if any, would be exempt from the tax and whether certain activities would qualify for credits under the tax. In general, the cost to the economy of achieving any given reduction in emissions could be minimized by limiting the number of entities that were exempt from paying the tax and by allowing tax credits for activities that capture and permanently store emissions before they are released.

Point of Implementation

The point at which a carbon tax was levied would have little bearing on the tax's ultimate effects on the economy and the environment. Thus, the decision about where to impose the tax could be based on the objective of covering the most emissions while minimizing the costs of implementing and complying with the tax. Achieving that goal would require identifying the points in the extraction-to-emissions path where fossil fuels are funneled through a relatively small number of entities and taking into account existing administrative structures that would make it easier to gather the data necessary for administering the tax.

---

4. For more about estimating the price of emission allowances, see Congressional Budget Office, *How CBO Estimates the Costs of Reducing Greenhouse-Gas Emissions* (April 2009), www.cbo.gov/publication/41745.

In general, levying a carbon tax relatively close to the point at which fossil fuels are extracted or imported would have the greatest likelihood of minimizing compliance costs and maximizing coverage.[5] That point varies for different fuels:

- In the case of petroleum, analysts conclude that it would be cost-effective to collect a carbon tax at the point at which petroleum is refined, because nearly all petroleum is processed by a limited number of refiners. Imposing a tax at that point would be facilitated by the fact that each barrel of crude oil that refiners receive is currently subject to a federal excise tax, whose revenues are directed to the Oil Spill Liability Trust Fund.

- In the case of coal, some analysts suggest that costs could be minimized, and coverage maximized, by imposing the tax on coal when it is mined (that is, implementing the tax at the mine mouth). Collecting a tax at that point would be made easier by the fact that coal producers are already subject to a federal excise tax, whose revenues are directed to the Black Lung Disability Trust Fund. Other analysts suggest that because the bulk of coal is used to generate electricity, emissions resulting from coal could be covered by taxing electricity generators on the basis of their actual emissions. Imposing the taxing at that point would be facilitated by the fact that the Environmental Protection Agency (EPA) collects data on CO_2 emissions by large generators.

- In the case of natural gas, some analysts suggest that costs could be minimized by levying the tax on operators of large natural gas wells or on natural gas processors. Alternatively, the tax could be implemented at the two points at which EPA collects data on natural-gas-related emissions under its Greenhouse Gas Reporting Program: when large generators use natural gas to produce electricity and when natural gas is sold to residential and commercial customers. (EPA collects data on those sales to cover emissions not related to electricity generation.)

Exemptions and Credits

Wherever a carbon tax was levied, subjecting all CO_2 emissions to the same tax rate would help ensure that the tax motivated businesses and households throughout the economy to undertake the least costly reductions in emissions, regardless of where or how those cuts might be achieved. For example, a tax of $20 per ton of emissions would raise the price of gasoline by about 20 cents per gallon; it would provide an incentive for firms and households to consume less gasoline, as long as the cost of doing so was less than the 20 cents per gallon saved. Exempting some sources of

---

5. For more details, see Gilbert E. Metcalf and David Wiesbach, "The Design of a Carbon Tax," *Harvard Environmental Law Review,* vol. 33, no. 2 (2009), pp. 499–556, http://tinyurl.com/bqgn46y; and Mandatory Reporting of Greenhouse Gases, 74 Fed. Reg. 56260 (October 30, 2009).

emissions (such as commercial vehicles) from the tax could prevent some low-cost reductions from being made.

If the tax was levied on the carbon content of fossil fuels, however, administrators could allow certain types of exemptions or tax credits without jeopardizing the goal of minimizing the cost of reducing emissions. In particular, noncombustive uses of fossil fuels—such as using petroleum to produce plastic or asphalt—could be exempt from the tax because they do not result in CO_2 emissions.

Researchers are working on technologies to capture and permanently store CO_2 emissions.[6] Designing a carbon tax to provide incentives for CO_2 capture and storage could be important if such technologies could reduce emissions at a per-ton cost that was lower than the tax rate. If the tax was levied on the actual emissions of electricity generators, for example, generators would have an incentive to reduce their tax payments by capturing and storing emissions. If the tax was levied on the carbon content of fossil fuels, however, the cost of the tax would be built into the price of fuels that generators purchased, so the tax would not give generators an incentive to store emissions. Lawmakers could create such an incentive by providing generators with an income tax credit for each ton of emissions that they captured and stored, with the value of the credit equal to the rate of the carbon tax. Administering a tax credit for CO_2 capture and storage would be made easier by the fact that large generators have equipment in place that continuously monitors their emissions. Administering tax credits for other activities that can capture carbon—such as preserving forests—would be much more complicated.[7]

Effects of a Carbon Tax on the Economy

Fossil fuels currently account for roughly 90 percent of all energy used in the United States, so taxing them would impose costs on the economy. The ultimate economic effects of a carbon tax, however, would depend on how the revenues from the tax were used. Some uses, such as reducing federal budget deficits or lowering existing marginal tax rates, would reduce the total costs to the economy from a carbon tax. Other uses would be unlikely to lower those total costs, but they could target relief to groups that would bear a disproportionate share of the burden from a carbon tax.

This report does not consider a comprehensive set of options for using the revenues from a carbon tax. Options not considered here include spending the revenues in ways that might also help the economy, such as investing in basic research and development or in education. Further, although this report focuses on a carbon tax, lawmakers could

---

6. See Congressional Budget Office, *Federal Efforts to Reduce the Cost of Capturing and Storing Carbon Dioxide* (June 2012), www.cbo.gov/publication/43357.

7. See Congressional Budget Office, *Deforestation and Greenhouse Gases* (January 2012), www.cbo.gov/publication/42686.

implement other policies that would both raise revenues and set a price on CO_2—such as a cap-and-trade program in which the government sold emission allowances rather than giving them to firms at no cost. A cap-and-trade program could provide more certainty about the overall amount of CO_2 emissions, which would be set by the cap, but it would provide less certainty about the price of emissions, which would depend on the cost of meeting the chosen cap.[8]

Economic Effects Without Accounting for the Use of the Tax Revenues

On its own—that is, not accounting for how its revenues were used—a carbon tax would affect the economy in many ways. Economists typically separate those effects into two components. "Primary" (or "resource") costs are the economic effects stemming directly from the carbon tax itself. "Tax-interaction" costs are the effects that result from the way in which a carbon tax would compound the economic costs associated with existing taxes, such as taxes on individual and corporate income. Those combined effects would be felt disproportionately by people in certain income groups, industries, and parts of the country.

Primary Costs. A carbon tax would increase the prices of fossil fuels in direct proportion to their carbon content. Higher fuel prices, in turn, would raise production costs and ultimately drive up prices for goods and services throughout the economy.[9] Prices of the most emission-intensive goods and services would rise by the largest amount. Thus, consumers would see the biggest price increases for items such as gasoline and electricity—particularly in areas where electricity is generated from coal, which produces the most CO_2 emissions per unit of power generated.

The changes in relative prices caused by the carbon tax (that is, the fact that some prices would increase more than others) would cause shifts in the goods and services

---

8. For a discussion of the similarities and differences between a carbon tax and a cap-and-trade program—and why either policy would generally be more efficient than setting standards that mandated the use of specific technologies or set firm-specific limits on emissions—see Congressional Budget Office, *Policy Options for Reducing CO_2 Emissions* (February 2008), www.cbo.gov/publication/41663. For a discussion of alternative approaches to reducing CO_2 emissions, see Alan Krupnick and Ian W.H. Parry, "What Is the Best Policy Instrument for Reducing CO_2 Emissions?" in Ian W.H. Parry, Ruud de Mooij, and Michael Keen, eds., *Fiscal Policy to Mitigate Climate Change: A Guide for Policymakers* (International Monetary Fund, 2012), pp. 1–25, http://tinyurl.com/cjnpaka.

9. For simplicity (unless otherwise noted), this discussion assumes that the costs of the tax would be passed on in full to consumers in the form of higher prices. If, in contrast, the Federal Reserve took actions to prevent that rise in prices, the relative prices of various goods and services would change because of the carbon tax, but the overall price level would remain constant. (Such actions by the Federal Reserve would not reduce the total long-run costs to the economy from a carbon tax; those costs would just not take the form of an increase in the overall price level.) In either case, the resulting shifts in production and consumption (and resulting changes in returns on capital and labor in various sectors of the economy) would be essentially the same in the long run. Finally, to the extent that pressure from imports prevented producers from passing price increases on to customers, the cost of the carbon tax would be directly borne by workers and investors.

that people buy—and in the way in which those goods and services are produced—that would lead to lower emissions. For example, the changes in relative prices would give households throughout the nation an incentive to reduce their consumption of electricity and gasoline, such as by installing more insulation, buying more-fuel-efficient appliances or vehicles, driving less, or taking public transportation. Likewise, manufacturers would have an incentive to produce goods in ways that resulted in fewer emissions, such as by generating electricity from natural gas or wind rather than from coal.

The primary costs of a carbon tax would consist mainly of two types of economic consequences: output effects and substitution effects. Output effects would occur when higher fossil-fuel prices reduced real wages and the profits on investment, causing the economy's total output to be lower than it would be otherwise. Substitution effects would occur when shifts in the mix of goods and services consumed, and in the way those goods and services were produced, changed the relative demand for labor and for physical capital (such as factories and heavy equipment used to produce electricity). Those changes would further affect real wages and profits on investment.

Output Effects. A carbon tax would reduce the economy's output by decreasing two things necessary to produce goods and services: the supply of labor and the amount of investment (see Figure 1).[10] In the case of labor, increases in fossil-fuel prices, and resulting increases in prices of goods and services, would diminish the purchasing power of people's earnings—that is, real wages would fall. The decline in real wages would have the net effect of causing people to work less, thus reducing the overall supply of labor.

The impact of lower real wages on the supply of labor is the net result of two countervailing forces: On the one hand, lower wages provide an incentive for people to work less and spend more time on activities that do not generate earnings—for example, one parent might choose to stay home with children rather than work outside the home because lower earnings would no longer make outside employment worthwhile. On the other hand, because lower wages reduce people's after-tax income, they create an incentive for people to work more to maintain the same standard of living. Research studies indicate that the first effect generally outweighs the second effect and that, overall, taxes that reduce real wages also reduce the labor supply.[11]

In the case of investment, increases in fossil-fuel prices because of a carbon tax would raise the cost of producing new physical capital. That increase in the cost of new

---

10. The reduction in output would have negative feedback effects on savings and the demand for labor, further reducing investment and real wages (not pictured in Figure 1).

11. For more details, see Congressional Budget Office, *How the Supply of Labor Responds to Changes in Fiscal Policy* (October 2012), www.cbo.gov/publication/43674.

capital would reduce the profits that the owners of capital earn on their investments, causing the overall level of investment to decline. (Lower returns on investment cause the same types of opposing forces described above for lower wages—they decrease the returns that people receive from saving and investing but increase the amount of saving and investing that people need to undertake to meet a given monetary goal. The first effect appears to generally outweigh the second, so taxes that reduce real returns on capital also reduce saving and investment.)

The decrease in investment could be muted to the extent that a carbon tax motivated companies to replace capital equipment earlier than they would otherwise, such as replacing a coal-fired power plant with a wind or nuclear power plant. Because the new capital would replace scrapped capital, however, it would not increase the productive capacity of the economy.

The generally negative impact on investment would begin when the carbon tax went into effect. Assuming that a significant delay occurred between when the tax was announced and when it took effect, anticipation of the tax might cause a slight increase in investment during the interim period if firms used that period to replace emission-intensive capital equipment. That additional investment could crowd out investment elsewhere in the economy. (Such crowding out would be greater the closer the economy was to operating at its maximum sustainable output during that interim period.)

Substitution Effects. In addition to their effects on output, increases in fossil-fuel prices caused by a carbon tax would lead consumers to switch from goods and services that involve relatively high emissions of carbon dioxide (and that would therefore experience larger price increases) to other goods and services that involve fewer CO_2 emissions. In addition, the tax would cause manufacturers to produce goods in ways that resulted in fewer emissions, primarily by cutting back on the use of fossil fuels in the production process. Those changes in the mix of products that people buy and in the way those products are made would cause labor and capital to shift throughout the economy and could alter the net flow of capital into or out of the United States. For example, in an attempt to reduce their use of fossil fuels, companies might switch to production methods that required more capital, relative to the amount of labor, per unit of output (such as by installing equipment that would more closely monitor and regulate energy use). That substitution would cause profits from investment to decline less—and real wages to decline more—than they would with only the output effects described above.[12]

---

12. For a discussion of conditions under which real wages could rise or fall relative to the returns on capital, see Don Fullerton and Garth Heutel, "The General Equilibrium Incidence of Environmental Taxes," *Journal of Public Economics,* vol. 91, nos. 3–4 (April 2007), pp. 571–591, http://dx.doi.org/10.1016/j.jpubeco.2006.07.004.

In theory, for a single factor of production, such as capital, substitution effects could more than fully offset the decline in returns caused by output effects (for example, causing the profits on investment to be higher than they would be without a carbon tax). In practice, however, such an outcome is unlikely and would require an even larger reduction in the returns on the other factor of production—in this case, wages. Thus, a carbon tax (excluding any use of its revenues) would be likely to reduce both real wages and profits on investment to some extent, but the relative changes in wages and profits would be uncertain.

A carbon tax would cause a smaller reduction in output if the cost of the tax fell on types of labor or capital that respond relatively little to changes in their prices. In particular, the decline in output would be lessened to the extent that the cost of the tax was borne by owners of existing stocks of fossil fuels (such as oil reserves and coal deposits) and by owners of existing fixed capital in emission-intensive industries (such as coal-fired power plants). Those owners would receive lower profits as a result of the tax, but because such resources were already in place, the supply of them would not change significantly in response to the carbon tax. Consequently, the effect on output would be diminished.

Although such an outcome would lessen the loss in output caused by the tax, it would also reduce the tax's impact on CO_2 emissions. Because part of the cost of the tax would be absorbed by owners of existing supplies of fossil fuels and fixed capital (in the form of lower profits), the price increases caused by the tax would be smaller than they would be if the full cost of the tax was passed on to consumers. As a result, businesses and households would have less incentive to reduce their emissions.[13]

Tax-Interaction Costs. The reductions in labor supply and investment caused by a carbon tax would compound the effects of current taxes that already discourage labor and investment (depicted in the lower portion of Figure 1), thereby increasing the negative effects on output.

Existing taxes on income—such as the corporate income tax, the individual income tax, and payroll taxes—create a gap between the amounts that companies pay for labor and capital and the after-tax amounts that workers and investors receive in the form of wages and returns on capital. The bigger that gap, the bigger the loss in output that would result from each additional increase in the tax rates on labor and investment. Such tax-interaction costs of a carbon tax could be large relative to the tax's primary costs.[14]

Burdens on Certain Groups. The burden of a carbon tax—that is, the hardship caused by price increases for fossil fuels and emission-intensive goods and services and by the

---

13. See Antonio M. Bento and Mark Jacobsen, "Ricardian Rents, Environmental Policy, and the 'Double-Dividend' Hypothesis," *Journal of Environmental Economics and Management*, vol. 53, no. 1 (January 2007), pp. 17–31, http://dx.doi.org/10.1016/j.jeem.2006.03.006.

reduction in wages and returns on investment—would fall disproportionately on several groups:

- Low-income households,

- Workers and investors in emission-intensive industries, and

- People in regions of the country that rely on emission-intensive industries for their livelihood or that use the most emission-intensive fuels to produce power.

The higher prices resulting from a carbon tax would tend to be regressive—that is, they would impose a larger burden (relative to income) on low-income households than on high-income households. The reason is that low-income households spend a larger share of their income on goods and services whose prices would increase the most, such as electricity and transportation. For example, an earlier CBO analysis concluded that a policy that set a price of $28 per metric ton on CO_2 emissions would increase costs for households by amounts that would equal about 2.5 percent of after-tax income for the average household in the lowest one-fifth (quintile) of the income distribution but less than 1 percent of after-tax income for the average household in the highest quintile.[15] Other analysts reached similar conclusions using a different method for allocating the cost of a carbon tax among households.[16] They estimated that the burden imposed by a tax of $20 per ton on CO_2 emissions would amount to 1.8 percent of before-tax income for households in the lowest quintile and about 0.7 percent of before-tax income for households in the highest quintile. A carbon tax would still be regressive, although less so, if the cost of the tax was measured relative to households' lifetime income rather than their annual income.[17]

---

14. See, for example, Ian W.H. Parry, Roberton C. Williams III, and Lawrence H. Goulder, "When Can Carbon Abatement Policies Increase Welfare? The Fundamental Role of Distorted Factor Markets," *Journal of Environmental Economics and Management,* vol. 37, no. 1 (January 1999), pp. 52–84, http://dx.doi.org/10.1006/jeem.1998.1058; Lawrence H. Goulder, "Environmental Policy Making in a Second-Best Setting," *Journal of Applied Economics,* vol. 1, no. 2 (1998), pp. 279–328; and A. Lans Bovenberg, "Green Tax Reforms and the Double Dividend: An Updated Reader's Guide," *International Tax and Public Finance,* vol. 6, no. 3 (August 1999), pp. 421–443, http://dx.doi.org/10.1023/A:1008715920337.

15. See Congressional Budget Office, *The Estimated Costs to Households From the Cap-and-Trade Provisions of H.R. 2454* (attachment to a letter to the Honorable Dave Camp, June 19, 2009), www.cbo.gov/publication/41194. Also see Terry Dinan, *Offsetting a Carbon Tax's Costs on Low-Income Households,* Working Paper 2012-16 (Congressional Budget Office, November 13, 2012), www.cbo.gov/publication/43713.

16. See Donald Marron and Eric Toder, *Carbon Taxes and Corporate Tax Reform* (Urban-Brookings Tax Policy Center, February 11, 2013), http://tinyurl.com/ctg57nv.

17. See Kevin A. Hasset, Aparna Mathur, and Gilbert E. Metcalf, "The Incidence of a U.S. Carbon Tax: A Lifetime and Regional Analysis," *Energy Journal,* vol. 30, no. 2 (2009), pp. 155–178, http://dx.doi.org/10.5547/ISSN0195-6574-EJ-Vol30-No2-8. That study used a proxy for households' lifetime income.

Workers and investors in fossil-fuel industries (such as coal mining and oil extraction) and in energy-intensive industries (such as chemicals, metals, and transportation) would tend to experience comparatively large losses in income under a carbon tax because demand for their products would decline. Specifically, CBO previously concluded that setting a price on CO_2 emissions would have the following effects on industries:

- Coal mining would be likely to experience the largest percentage decline in employment.

- Employment in oil and gas extraction and natural gas utilities would probably also decline—though to a smaller extent, in percentage terms, than employment in coal mining.

- Other types of mining, construction, transportation, and the industries that produce metals, nonmetallic mineral products (such as glass), and chemicals—all of which use relatively large amounts of energy directly or indirectly—would probably also see their employment decrease, although the percentage declines would be relatively small.[18]

Declines in such industries would be offset, over time, by increases in employment in industries and sectors (such as services) whose products are less emission-intensive to produce and result in fewer emissions when used. Employment would also increase in industries that manufacture equipment to produce energy from low-emission sources, such as nuclear, solar, and wind power.

The effects of a carbon tax would vary by region as well. Parts of the country that rely on fossil fuels or energy-intensive production for income would experience larger losses than other regions. Likewise, households in places where electricity is generated from coal would probably see larger increases in electricity prices than their counterparts in other regions. For example, analysts have estimated that a tax of about $21 per metric ton on CO_2 emissions would raise the price of electricity by an average of 16 percent for the United States as a whole, but that increase would vary widely in different parts of the country.[19] Households in Illinois, Indiana, Kentucky, Michigan, Missouri, Ohio, West Virginia, and Wisconsin would see the biggest rise in electricity prices (27 percent), and households in California would see the smallest rise (7 percent). Including all of the price increases associated with a carbon tax, not just increases in electricity prices,

---

18. See Congressional Budget Office, *How Policies to Reduce Greenhouse Gas Emissions Could Affect Employment* (May 2010), www.cbo.gov/publication/41257, and *The Economic Effects of Legislation to Reduce Greenhouse-Gas Emissions* (September 2009), www.cbo.gov/publication/41266.

19. See Dallas Burtraw, Richard Sweeney, and Margaret Walls, "The Incidence of U.S. Climate Policy: Alternative Uses of Revenues from a Cap-and-Trade Auction," *National Tax Journal*, vol. 62, no. 3 (September 2009), pp. 497–518, http://ntj.tax.org.

would imply a somewhat different geographic pattern, because areas that have relatively few emissions from electricity generation may have sizable emissions from other sources, such as vehicles.

Economic Effects Related to the Use of the Tax Revenues

Lawmakers could use the revenues from a carbon tax in numerous ways, including to reduce federal budget deficits, to decrease existing marginal tax rates, or to compensate people who would bear a disproportionate share of the cost of the carbon tax. Each of those uses would have different effects on the economy.

In general, decisions about how to use the revenues would not affect incentives for businesses and households to make cuts in emissions that could be achieved at a cost below that of the tax. An exception would occur if firms or households received compensation that was linked to their consumption of fossil fuels. In that case, using more fossil fuels would increase their compensation, undermining incentives to cut emissions.

Using the Revenues to Reduce the Deficit. Once the economy has returned to its maximum sustainable level of output, persistent budget deficits would crowd out some private-sector investment, which would slow the growth of the economy's output and people's income. In addition, the mounting federal debt that would result from those deficits would require rising federal interest payments, restrict lawmakers' ability to use fiscal policy to respond to unexpected challenges, and increase the probability of a sudden fiscal crisis.[20]

Policies that trimmed deficits would mitigate such adverse economic consequences by increasing national saving and investment, thus leading to an increase in output in the long run.[21] If a carbon tax was used to reduce future budget deficits, the long-term effect on total output would depend on the relative sizes of two offsetting factors: the negative effects of the tax itself (which would reduce real wages, investment, and output) and the positive effects of accumulating less debt than would otherwise be the case (which would increase real wages, investment, and output).

CBO has not estimated how a carbon tax combined with a deficit reduction policy would affect output. However, an earlier CBO analysis concluded that eliminating various tax cuts enacted in 2001 and 2003 would have boosted output in the long term: The reduction in output caused by those tax changes would ultimately have been

---

20. For more discussion, see Congressional Budget Office, *The 2012 Long-Term Budget Outlook* (June 2012), www.cbo.gov/publication/43288.

21. See Congressional Budget Office, *The Macroeconomic and Budgetary Effects of an Illustrative Policy for Reducing the Federal Budget Deficit* (July 2011), www.cbo.gov/publication/41580.

more than offset by the increase in output brought about by having smaller deficits.[22] Eliminating those tax cuts would have involved raising marginal income tax rates and making a variety of other changes to the tax code, some of which would not have altered marginal income tax rates and thus would have tended to have fewer harmful effects on the economy. If a carbon tax was more costly to the economy than the package of tax changes that CBO considered, using it to reduce deficits would have a smaller positive effect—or a net negative effect—on output in the long term. Different analyses of using a carbon tax to reduce federal debt could reach different conclusions about the net economic effect.[23]

Using the Revenues to Reduce Existing Marginal Tax Rates. Current taxes on individual and corporate income generally decrease households' after-tax returns from working, saving, and investing. Those lower returns reduce the overall supply of labor and capital, leading to less economic output than would otherwise be the case. As described above, a carbon tax would compound the effects of those existing taxes, potentially creating significant tax-interaction costs.

Using the revenues from a carbon tax to reduce existing marginal tax rates—an approach called a tax swap—would diminish the economic costs of the tax. The net effect of a tax swap on output would depend on the relative sizes of the loss in output caused by the carbon tax itself (including both the primary costs and the tax-interaction costs) and the gain in output caused by the reduction in existing marginal tax rates.

CBO has not quantified the effects of a tax swap. However, various studies that have looked at different types of tax swaps have concluded that a well-designed swap would significantly lower the economic costs of a carbon tax, and a few studies have concluded that a tax swap could lead to a net increase in output. A well-designed tax swap would cut marginal tax rates (the rates on an additional dollar of income), thereby raising the after-tax returns that people receive from work or investment and leading to increases in those activities.

---

22. That analysis found that cutting income tax rates and increasing deficits would lead to lower output; correspondingly, reducing deficits would increase output. See the testimony of Douglas W. Elmendorf, Director, Congressional Budget Office, before the Senate Committee on the Budget, *The Economic Outlook and Fiscal Policy Choices* (September 28, 2010), www.cbo.gov/publication/21836.

23. One recent study estimated that reducing federal debt by using revenues from a carbon tax (with a rate of $15 per ton of CO_2 emissions in 2012, rising by 4 percent above inflation each year) would cause output to be lower throughout the first 40 years of the policy than it would be without such a policy. See Warwick J. McKibbin and others, *The Potential Role of a Carbon Tax in U.S. Fiscal ZReform*, Climate and Energy Economics Discussion Paper (Brookings Institution, July 24, 2012), http://tinyurl.com/btkd5xf. That study accounted for some, but not all, of the potential effects that lower federal debt could have on the economy. For example, it accounted for the fact that a smaller debt would reduce the government's interest payments (holding the interest rate constant), but it did not include the possibility that failing to reduce the debt could increase the interest rates that the United States would face to borrow funds.

Different studies reach different conclusions about the extent to which a tax swap would offset the costs of a carbon tax.[24] For example, one study examined the impact of using carbon tax revenues to fund several specific tax cuts—including reductions in marginal rates for payroll taxes, corporate income taxes, and individual income taxes.[25] It concluded that the reduction in output caused by the carbon tax would be larger than the increase in output caused by the accompanying tax cuts, although that net reduction in output would be nearly 50 percent less than if the revenues were returned to households in a way that did not increase their incentives to work and invest.

Another, more recent study concluded that using the revenues from a carbon tax to pay for a cut in marginal tax rates on capital (modeled as a generic tax cut on all capital rather than as a cut in a specific type of tax on capital) would cause output to be higher for several decades than it would be without the carbon tax and corresponding tax cut.[26] That study also estimated that cutting marginal tax rates on labor would help limit the reduction in output caused by a carbon tax (relative to the case in which the revenues were returned to households in a manner that did not increase incentives to work or invest) but that the net effect of the carbon tax and tax swap on output would still be negative.[27] Another recent study estimated that using half of the revenues from a carbon tax to reduce the deficit and the other half to reduce marginal tax rates on individual income would lead to lower output throughout the 50-year period examined.[28]

Thus, although many researchers agree that a tax swap could limit the economic costs of a carbon tax, they differ in their estimates of how far the tax swap would go to offset those costs, for at least three reasons. One source of such differences is the details of the tax swaps that researchers examine. Taxes vary in terms of how they affect different

---

24. To determine the extent to which a tax swap would decrease the tax-interaction costs, researchers typically compare the economic effects of a tax swap with the economic effects of a policy that would use carbon tax revenues in a way that would not increase people's incentives to work or invest.

25. See Lawrence H. Goulder, "Effects of Carbon Taxes in an Economy With Prior Tax Distortions: An Intertemporal General Equilibrium Analysis," *Journal of Environmental Economics and Management,* vol. 29, no. 3 (November 1995), pp. 271–297, http://dx.doi.org/10.1006/jeem.1995.1047.

26. See Warwick J. McKibbin and others, *The Potential Role of a Carbon Tax in U.S. Fiscal Reform,* Climate and Energy Economics Discussion Paper (Brookings Institution, July 24, 2012), http://tinyurl.com/btkd5xf.

27. Another recent study looked at how tax swaps would affect the discounted present value of the remaining lifetime consumption of households representing different generations. It concluded that most generations would be better off if carbon tax revenues were used to cut taxes on capital than if they were used to cut taxes on labor or consumption. See Jared C. Carbone, Richard D. Morgenstern, and Roberton C. Williams III, "Carbon Taxes and Deficit Reduction" (draft, May 2012), www.econ.gatech.edu/files/seminars/Williams.pdf (2.3 MB).

28. See Anne E. Smith and others, *Economic Outcomes of a U.S. Carbon Tax* (report prepared by NERA Economic Consulting for the National Association of Manufacturers, February 17, 2013), www.nera.com/67_8014.htm.

types of capital and labor, so the outcomes of studies depend crucially on the details of the policies being analyzed.

Another source of differences among studies is that researchers evaluate policies according to different measures. Some studies, including those described above, report effects on output. Others evaluate policies relative to other measures, such as effects on "welfare" (which researchers typically define as the change in the value of consumption and leisure). One set of researchers, using welfare as a measure, concluded that using carbon tax revenues to fund cuts in marginal tax rates on corporate income, individual income, or wages would increase welfare over the first decade of the policy.[29] That estimated increase in welfare does not imply that output would also be higher, because welfare and output can differ; for example, increases in leisure could increase welfare but reduce output.

Finally, researchers who evaluate similar policies according to similar measures can obtain different results because of differences in the models they use. Such differences can involve the way in which models account for effects on international trade, the extent to which they distinguish among different types of capital, the level of detail about existing taxes, and assumptions about the degree to which labor and capital respond to changes in their after-tax prices.

Using the Revenues to Offset Effects on Certain Groups. As noted above, the burden of a carbon tax would fall disproportionately on low-income households, workers and investors in emission-intensive industries, and people in areas where the local economy relies on such industries or on electricity generated from emission-intensive fuels. Lawmakers could partly or fully offset the burden imposed on those groups by returning some or most of the carbon tax revenues to them through tax credits or other programs. For example, carbon tax revenues could be directed to low-income households in the form of fixed (lump-sum) payments. (Households who are eligible for benefits under the Supplemental Nutrition Assistance Program, formerly known as the Food Stamp program, could receive an additional fixed amount of benefits, for

---

29. See Sebastian Rausch and John Reilly, *Carbon Tax Revenue and the Budget Deficit: A Win-Win-Win Solution?* Report 228 (Massachusetts Institute of Technology Joint Program on the Science and Policy of Global Change, August 2012), http://tinyurl.com/cvx3bl9. Other analysts have examined how changes in marginal taxes on income can affect welfare by reducing changes in consumption caused by tax preferences. For example, the tax deduction for mortgage interest causes people to spend more on housing than they might otherwise. A reduction in marginal taxes on income would reduce the value of the mortgage interest deduction and thus the extent to which the tax system alters people's choices about consumption. See Ian W.H. Parry and Roberton C. Williams III, "What Are the Costs of Meeting Distributional Objectives for Climate Policy?" *B.E. Journal of Economic Analysis & Policy,* vol. 10, no. 2 (December 2010), http://tinyurl.com/d8frxk4. For more about the effects of tax-preferred consumption, see Ian W.H. Parry and Antonio M. Bento, "Tax Deductions, Environmental Policy, and the 'Double Dividend' Hypothesis," *Journal of Environmental Economics and Management,* vol. 39, no. 1 (January 2000), pp. 67–96, http://dx.doi.org/10.1006/jeem.1999.1093.

instance.) Such payments could help offset the increase in living expenses that those households would experience because of a carbon tax.[30]

However, unlike using carbon tax revenues to reduce deficits or marginal tax rates, using them to provide relief from the tax's effects on certain groups would generally not lessen the total economic costs of a carbon tax, including the reduction in total output. For example, lump-sum payments to low-income households would not provide benefits to the broader economy under normal economic conditions, because those payments would not increase people's incentives to work or invest and thus would not lead to greater economic productivity.[31] Conversely, using the revenues to cut marginal tax rates on corporate or individual income would benefit the economy more broadly but would probably have limited value to low-income households, who typically owe little, if any, income tax. As a result, lawmakers could face a trade-off between using carbon tax revenues to minimize the tax's adverse effects on the economy as a whole and using them to minimize the tax's impact on disproportionately affected groups.

Lawmakers could balance those trade-offs by choosing to use the revenues in more than one way. For instance, they could allocate some of the revenues to offsetting costs for hard-hit households and the rest to reducing economywide costs. By one estimate, offsetting the costs of a carbon tax for households in the lowest two-fifths of the income distribution would take less than 30 percent of the gross revenues from a carbon tax; offsetting the costs for households in the lowest one-fifth of the income distribution would take roughly 12 percent.[32]

---

30. For more discussion of that and other options for helping households who would bear relatively large costs, see Congressional Budget Office, *How Policies to Reduce Greenhouse Gas Emissions Could Affect Employment* (May 2010), www.cbo.gov/publication/41257, and *Options for Offsetting the Economic Impact on Low- and Moderate-Income Households of a Cap-and-Trade Program for Carbon Dioxide Emissions* (attachment to a letter to the Honorable Jeff Bingaman, June 17, 2008), www.cbo.gov/publication/41704; testimony of Terry M. Dinan, Senior Advisor, Congressional Budget Office, before the Subcommittee on Income Security and Family Support of the House Committee on Ways and Means, *The Distributional Consequences of a Cap-and-Trade Program for CO_2 Emissions* (March 12, 2009), www.cbo.gov/publication/41168; and testimony of Douglas W. Elmendorf, Director, Congressional Budget Office, before the Senate Committee on Finance, *The Distribution of Revenues from a Cap-and-Trade Program for CO_2 Emissions* (May 7, 2009), www.cbo.gov/publication/41183. Households that received compensation would still have an incentive to reduce emissions only if the compensation they received was unrelated to the amount of energy they used.

31. Limiting lump-sum rebates to households below a certain income level could provide a disincentive to work.

32. See Terry Dinan, *Offsetting a Carbon Tax's Costs on Low-Income Households*, Working Paper 2012-16 (Congressional Budget Office, November 2012), www.cbo.gov/publication/43713.

Effects of a Carbon Tax on the Environment

Imposing a federal carbon tax would reduce the expected environmental and economic damage from climate change by lowering CO_2 emissions in the United States. Calculating the value of reduced damage is fraught with scientific and economic uncertainties, and estimates of that value span a wide range. Moreover, the United States accounts for less than one-fifth of global CO_2 emissions, so reductions in emissions in this country would probably have only a modest effect on the Earth's climate unless they were part of a coordinated effort with other countries. Still, cuts in U.S. emissions alone would produce incremental reductions in expected damage, and coordinated cuts in emissions would reduce the risk of costly—potentially catastrophic—damage.

The Impact of CO_2 Emissions

Since the onset of the industrial revolution more than two centuries ago, people have released increasing quantities of greenhouse gases into the atmosphere—the main one being carbon dioxide, which is emitted when fossil fuels are burned. Global fossil-fuel-related emissions of CO_2 are expected to grow substantially in the coming decades: by 35 percent between 2012 and 2035.[33]

Rising CO_2 emissions cause concern because they, along with other greenhouse gases, accumulate in the atmosphere—potentially remaining there for centuries—and trap the sun's heat, causing average temperatures on Earth to rise. The extent of that warming is unclear, but under a range of plausible alternative assumptions, many studies project that the total amount of warming that might occur during the 200 years from 1900 to 2100 would be a substantial fraction of the amount of warming that occurred over an 8,000-year period at the end of the last ice age (between 18,000 and 10,000 years ago).

The consequences of rising global temperatures are highly uncertain and are projected to vary widely throughout the United States and the rest of the world. However, rising temperatures are expected to be costly overall. Among the less uncertain effects on humans, some would be positive, such as reduced deaths from cold weather and improvements in agricultural productivity in certain areas; others would be negative, such as declines in the availability of fresh water in areas dependent on snow melt and loss of property from storm surges as sea levels rise.[34]

Among the more uncertain outcomes, of particular concern is whether warming will cause shifts in regional patterns of temperature and rainfall that are relatively sudden and unexpected, thus limiting opportunities for people and ecosystems to adjust. Sharp

---

33. See Energy Information Administration, *International Energy Outlook 2011*, DOE/EIA-0484 (2011) (September 2011), www.eia.gov/forecasts/ieo/emissions.cfm.

34. See Congressional Budget Office, *Potential Impacts of Climate Change in the United States* (May 2009), www.cbo.gov/publication/41180.

increases in damage would be particularly likely if rising temperatures triggered events—such as the release of methane, a potent greenhouse gas currently trapped in permafrost—that in turn accelerated the pace of warming.

The International Context

Both the causes and the consequences of climate change are global. The effects of such change would be experienced around the world, and significantly limiting the increase in global temperatures would require efforts by multiple countries.

Many nations, including the United States, have already taken some steps to reduce greenhouse gas emissions. Those steps involve a variety of approaches, including regulations (such as fuel-efficiency standards for automobiles) and incentives (such as subsidies for zero- or low-emitting technologies). A few countries have enacted policies that set a price on CO_2 emissions; most notably, 27 member nations of the European Union, along with the 3 other members of the European Economic Area, have established a cap-and-trade program for greenhouse gas emissions.[35] In total, however, global efforts to date are expected to fall well short of the reductions necessary to prevent emissions from climbing to levels that would lead to significant increases in average global temperatures.

The United States currently accounts for about 18 percent of global CO_2 emissions; that share is projected to decline to about 15 percent by 2035 as emissions in other countries rise. Acting on its own, the United States could have only a modest effect on the amount of warming. In particular, efforts to limit global warming are likely to require significant reductions in emissions by rapidly growing economies, such as those of China and India.

A coordinated, global approach to cutting emissions would also reduce the extent to which some of the decrease in U.S. emissions resulting from a federal carbon tax would be offset by increases in emissions overseas—a phenomenon known as carbon leakage. Analysts have estimated that in the absence of a global approach, between 1 percent and 23 percent of the reduction in U.S. emissions stemming from a U.S. carbon tax (or similar policy) could be offset through leakage, as higher prices for emission-intensive goods produced in the United States increased demand for cheaper emission-intensive goods produced elsewhere. The United States could address some types of leakage through policies, such as tariffs, that would impose the same costs on imports of emission-intensive goods that a carbon tax would impose on U.S. production of those goods; however, practical and legal challenges to such policies

---

35. See Richard G. Newell, William A. Pizer, and Daniel Raimi, "Carbon Markets 15 Years After Kyoto: Lessons Learned, New Challenges," *Journal of Economic Perspectives*, vol. 27, no. 1 (Winter 2013), pp. 123–146, http://dx.doi.org/10.1257/jep.27.1.123; and Jane A. Leggett and others, *An Overview of Greenhouse Gas (GHG) Control Policies in Various Countries*, Report for Congress R40936 (Congressional Research Service, November 30, 2009).

could limit their effectiveness.[36] Alternatively, in the case of a cap-and-trade program, analysts have proposed reducing the extent to which the production of emission-intensive goods would shift overseas by providing U.S. producers in those industries with free emission allowances based on their level of production. (Such a policy would limit increases in the U.S. prices of those goods and thus limit shifts in production.) That approach could also face legal challenges. Addressing the same concerns through a carbon tax would entail providing such producers with a tax rebate that was linked to their output.

Assessing the Value of Incremental Reductions in CO_2 Emissions

Although significantly limiting the amount of warming that might occur would require a concerted effort by major emitting countries, incremental reductions in emissions would cause incremental reductions in the expected damage from climate change. Researchers have produced estimates of the monetary value of the future damage from climate change associated with an increase of one metric ton in CO_2 emissions in a given year—a measure often referred to as the social cost of carbon. That measure also approximates the expected benefit, in terms of avoided future damage, associated with a commensurate decrease in emissions. Because the SCC reflects the expected global benefit of an incremental change in CO_2 emissions, it reflects the value that each 1-ton reduction in U.S. emissions would have, assuming no changes in emissions outside the United States.

Estimates of the social cost of carbon are highly uncertain. Producing such estimates entails predicting the degree of warming that might result from rising global emissions of greenhouse gases, estimating the range of global effects (both positive and negative) that such warming might have, placing a dollar value on those effects in various years, and translating future dollar values into current ones. Researchers have made such estimates using models that combine simplified representations of the climate system, the global economy, and the way in which those two interact. Given the uncertainties involved, researchers typically calculate a range of estimates for the SCC using alternative assumptions about key parameters.

In 2009, the U.S. government formed an interagency working group to develop estimates of the social cost of carbon to be used in analyzing potential federal regulations. That effort offers insights into the uncertainties underlying such estimates and the important role of particular parameters. In estimating the SCC, the working group used three different models; five different scenarios about projections of global economic output, population, and emissions; and three different discount rates to translate future values into present values (higher discount rates give less weight to

---

36. For further discussion, see Environmental Protection Agency and others, *The Effects of H.R. 2454 on International Competitiveness and Emission Leakage in Energy-Intensive Trade-Exposed Industries: An Interagency Report Responding to a Request from Senators Bayh, Specter, Stabenow, McCaskill, and Brown* (December 2, 2009), http://go.usa.gov/2unQ (pdf, 1 MB).

future values than lower discount rates do).[37] In total, those combinations provided 45 different estimates of the social cost of carbon for any given year. Because the outcomes are uncertain, each of those 45 estimates was represented as a probability distribution (a range of possible outcomes with weights attached to each one).

The working group reported average estimates for the SCC in a given year for each of the three discount rates. (Those estimates were averages of the 15 outcomes that resulted from applying the five scenarios to each of the three models.) For 2010, for instance, the working group concluded that the average estimate for the SCC could be as low as $5 per ton of CO_2 emissions (in 2007 dollars) or as high as $35, depending on the discount rate that was applied to future outcomes (see Table 1). The working group described the average value calculated using a 3 percent discount rate as the "central estimate" for each year; for 2010, the central estimate was $21 per ton.[38]

Because much of the concern about climate change focuses on the potential for extreme damage, the working group also reported the potential for the social cost of carbon to be well above the average estimate indicated by the models. In particular, using the 3 percent discount rate and averaging across its three models, the working group estimated that there was a 5 percent chance that the true value of the SCC in 2010—that is, the actual global damage that would result from CO_2 emissions—could exceed $65 per ton (not shown in Table 1).

Importance of Discount Rates. The interagency working group's average estimate of the SCC for 2010 varied by a factor of seven (from $5 to $35) depending on the rate at which future damage was discounted. Today's emissions produce effects that will unfold over decades, even centuries; thus, estimates of the present value of the damage resulting from today's emissions are highly sensitive to the weight put on future damage.

The choice of a discount rate not only affects the initial value of the SCC but also helps determine the rate at which the SCC increases over time (rising SCC values reflect rising estimates of damage). Higher discount rates result in lower initial values of the SCC but, according to the working group's models, faster subsequent growth in those values. For example, the working group estimated that with a 3 percent discount rate, the SCC would increase by roughly 2 percent a year over the first four decades, but

---

37. A present value is a single number that expresses a flow of future costs in terms of an equivalent lump-sum cost today. The present value depends on the interest rate, called the discount rate, that is used to translate future cash flows into current dollars.

38. See Interagency Working Group on Social Cost of Carbon, *Technical Support Document: Social Cost of Carbon for Regulatory Impact Analysis Under Executive Order 12866* (February 2010), http://go.usa.gov/2une (pdf, 847 KB); and Charles Griffiths and others, "The Social Cost of Carbon: Valuing Carbon Reductions in Policy Analysis," in Ian W.H. Parry, Ruud de Mooij, and Michael Keen, eds., *Fiscal Policy to Mitigate Climate Change: A Guide for Policymakers* (International Monetary Fund, 2012), pp. 69–87, http://tinyurl.com/cjnpaka.

with a 5 percent discount rate, it would grow by roughly 3 percent a year over that period.

Importance of Catastrophic Effects and Adaptation. The three models used by the interagency working group illustrate the importance to the social cost of carbon of the potential for catastrophic effects—generally represented as a substantial loss in global output—and of the ability of humans and ecosystems to adapt to a changing climate. Models that make different assumptions about those factors produce very different estimates of the SCC.

The sensitivity of estimates to those assumptions is revealed by comparing the three models' estimates of the expected loss in global output that would occur if average surface temperatures increased by 2.5°C from their preindustrial levels. One model estimated that such warming would reduce global output by 1.5 percent, with nearly 70 percent of that expected loss stemming from the small probability that the warming would trigger a catastrophic loss (defined as a 25 percent decline in global output). Another model, which did not include the potential for catastrophic effects, estimated that 2.5°C of warming would be beneficial, on net, raising global output by 0.13 percent (mainly because of increases in productivity in the agricultural and forestry sectors and decreases in heating costs). The third model assumed that humans and ecosystems would adapt to gradual warming and that damage would occur only above a "tolerable level" (defined as 2°C of warming). That model estimated that 2.5°C of warming would reduce expected global output by 1.44 percent, with roughly 30 percent of that decline caused by the small probability of a catastrophic loss.[39]

Non-CO_2-Related Benefits and Costs. Although the social cost of carbon reflects reductions in the expected damage and risks posed by climate change, cutting CO_2 emissions could have other effects as well. In particular, researchers have examined how efforts to lower CO_2 emissions—such as generating electricity from natural gas rather than from coal—might also lower emissions of other gases. Reduced emissions of those pollutants would create additional benefits (sometimes referred to as co-benefits, or ancillary benefits). Co-benefits could include a variety of effects, such as reduced incidences of asthma and premature death. Conversely, measures taken to decrease CO_2 emissions could create additional costs depending on how the emissions were reduced. Estimating the net change in damage, or the net co-benefit,

---

39. The three models are the Dynamic Integrated Climate Economy (DICE) model, the Climate Framework for Uncertainty, Negotiations, and Distribution (FUND) model, and the Policy Analysis for the Greenhouse Effect (PAGE) model, respectively. See Charles Griffiths and others, "The Social Cost of Carbon: Valuing Carbon Reductions in Policy Analysis," in Ian W.H. Parry, Ruud de Mooij, and Michael Keen, eds., *Fiscal Policy to Mitigate Climate Change: A Guide for Policymakers* (International Monetary Fund, 2012), pp. 69–87, http://tinyurl.com/cjnpaka. Different models define catastrophic outcomes in different ways. For example, the DICE model defines it as a 25 percent loss in global output as measured by gross domestic product. See William D. Nordhaus and Joseph Boyer, *Warming the World: Economic Models of Global Warming* (Massachusetts Institute of Technology Press, 2000), http://mitpress.mit.edu/books/warming-world.

that might result from a carbon tax becomes more complicated if analysts take into account the entire process of fuel production, use, and disposal. For example, to the extent that the tax caused generators to shift away from coal to nuclear power, it could decrease the damage stemming from coal mining but increase the risks associated with disposing of nuclear waste.

Some analysts have estimated that certain co-benefits of a carbon tax could be significant, but those co-benefits (as well as potential additional damage) would depend on how CO_2 emissions were reduced and on what standards were already in place to limit other emissions. For example, one recent study concluded that a carbon tax of $29 (rising by 5 percent more than inflation each year) would yield health-related co-benefits of about $10 per ton of CO_2 emissions reduced—or more than twice that amount depending on whether the carbon tax caused electricity generators' emissions of sulfur dioxide to decline.[40] Whether that decline occurred would, in turn, depend on whether an existing regulatory cap on sulfur dioxide emissions was binding and whether regulations to tighten the cap were enacted.[41]

Determining the Tax Rate That Best Balances the Benefits and Costs of a Carbon Tax

In theory, if there were no other taxes, no leakage from emissions elsewhere, no non-CO_2-related benefits or costs (beyond the net environmental costs reflected in the social cost of carbon and the primary economic costs of a carbon tax described above), and no uncertainty about the SCC, then setting the rate of a carbon tax equal to the SCC would be "efficient" from a global economic standpoint. That is, it would ensure that the economic costs (as reflected in the primary costs) of the most expensive emission cuts prompted by the tax would equal the net environmental benefits of those cuts. For example, if lawmakers chose $21 as an appropriate estimate for the SCC, setting the carbon tax at that rate would prompt firms and households to reduce emissions as long as the per-ton cost of making those reductions was less than $21— and thus, the most expensive emission cuts made as a result of a tax would cost no more than the estimated damage avoided by those cuts.

In practice, however, the carbon tax rate that is economically efficient depends on the way in which lawmakers use the revenues from the tax, the amount of leakage that occurs, and the amount of additional benefits and costs that result from the tax.

---

40. See Britt Groosman, Nicholas Z. Muller, and Erin O'Neill-Toy, "The Ancillary Benefits from Climate Policy in the United States," *Environmental and Resource Economics,* vol. 50, no. 4 (December 2011), pp. 585–603, http://dx.doi.org/10.1007/s10640-011-9483-9. (The estimates are in 2006 dollars.)

41. In recent years, emissions of sulfur dioxide (SO_2) have fallen below the level of the cap imposed by EPA's Acid Rain Program, so that cap does not appear to be binding at present. EPA set a more stringent cap on SO_2 emissions under the Cross State Air Pollution Rule, but that rule was struck down by the D.C. Circuit Court in August 2012. EPA is currently appealing that decision.

Moreover, some analysts say that estimates of the SCC may be too uncertain to be a useful guide to setting a tax rate. (Some analysts suggest instead that the tax could be set at a rate that would be projected to keep atmospheric CO_2 from exceeding a particular concentration.) In addition, economic efficiency is only one of the criteria that lawmakers might use in setting that rate.

Alternative Uses of the Tax Revenues. Because a carbon tax would compound the costs associated with current taxes on individual and corporate income, the incremental cost to the economy from a carbon tax would exceed the actual rate of the tax. Thus, with a tax of $21 per ton of CO_2 (not counting the use of the tax revenues), the most expensive emission cuts would have a combined primary and tax-interaction cost of more than $21.

If the revenues from the carbon tax were used in ways that did not offset that compounding effect—for example, if they were distributed to all U.S. residents on an equal, lump-sum basis—the economically efficient level of the tax would probably be less than the social cost of carbon. Alternatively, to the extent that lawmakers used the carbon tax revenues in ways that offset the tax's negative effects on real wages, investment, and output, the efficient level of the tax would be closer to—or perhaps even greater than—the SCC.

Potential for Leakage. The benefits of a U.S. carbon tax would be reduced to the extent that decreases in emissions in the United States were expected to be offset by increases in emissions outside the United States. In that case, the tax rate that would be economically efficient would be lower than the social cost of carbon, to reflect offsetting increases in emissions elsewhere. For example, if 10 percent of the total decrease in U.S. emissions was expected to be offset by increases overseas, the value of each 1-ton reduction in U.S. emissions would be 10 percent less than the SCC (which represents the value of a 1-ton reduction in global emissions). Unless a U.S. carbon tax was part of a coordinated global effort or was accompanied by measures to prevent leakage, increases in emissions elsewhere would offset 1 percent to 23 percent of the reduction in U.S. emissions, analysts estimate.

Additional Non-CO_2-Related Benefits and Costs. If a carbon tax had benefits unrelated to reducing the risk of climate change or had costs other than the primary and tax-interaction costs discussed above, the net value of those benefits and costs (the net co-benefit) could be added to estimates of the social cost of carbon when considering what carbon tax rate would be economically efficient. Although most researchers have estimated positive values for the net co-benefit, suggesting an efficient tax rate higher than the SCC, the net co-benefit could, at least in theory, be negative, suggesting an efficient tax rate lower than the SCC.

Modifying the chosen tax rate to reflect the net co-benefit would be complicated, however, by the fact that the size of the net co-benefit would vary depending on how cuts in CO_2 emissions were achieved. Some methods of reducing CO_2 emissions could have a significantly larger net co-benefit than others would, and the magnitude of that co-benefit would change over time as the methods used in response to the tax changed. Thus, modifying the tax to reflect the average net co-benefit could provide too much incentive for changes in some types of production and consumption and too little incentive for changes in other types. Using separate policy instruments to address separate environmental problems reflected in the net co-benefit—such as emissions of various pollutants—would generally be more efficient than addressing such problems together with climate change through a carbon tax.

Uncertainty of Estimates of the Social Cost of Carbon. Estimates of the SCC have the potential to incorporate a degree of uncertainty about the environmental damage from CO_2 emissions and people's aversion to the risk of such damage.[42] However, some researchers suggest that the unknown potential of climate change to trigger catastrophic outcomes—as well as the great uncertainty associated with estimating the likelihood and magnitude of those outcomes—severely limits analysts' ability to produce meaningful estimates of the SCC. Some argue that the plausible range of incremental damage is much larger than typically presented, that little evidence exists to dismiss very large potential values (although values below the central estimates discussed above are also possible), and that the types of models typically used to estimate the social cost of carbon do not adequately capture the extent of the underlying uncertainties.[43] According to that view, estimates of the SCC that result from models such as those used by the interagency working group could be of limited use to lawmakers in setting a carbon tax rate.

The Timing of Action

Because the damage from climate change depends on the amount of emissions that accumulate over a long period of time, rather than the level of emissions in any one year, some analysts suggest that delaying reductions in emissions might be beneficial.[44] In particular, they suggest that emissions could be cut more cheaply in the future, for several reasons:

- Technological improvements might reduce the cost of lower-emission methods of producing goods, even in the absence of policies designed to encourage fewer

42. See William Nordhaus, *Estimates of the Social Cost of Carbon: Background and Results from the RICE-2011 Model,* Cowles Foundation Discussion Paper 1826 (Yale University, October 2011), http://dido.econ.yale.edu/P/cd/d18a/d1826.pdf (370 KB).

43. See, for example, Martin L. Weitzman, "Fat-Tailed Uncertainty in the Economics of Catastrophic Climate Change," *Review of Environmental Economics and Policy,* vol. 5, no. 2 (Summer 2011), pp. 275–292, http://dx.doi.org/10.1093/reep/rer006; and Geoffrey Heal and Antony Millner, *Uncertainty and Decision in Climate Change Economics,* Working Paper 18929 (National Bureau of Economic Research, March 2013), www.nber.org/papers/w18929.

44. See, for example, Robert P. Murphy, *Carbon "Tax Swap" Deals: A Review and Critique* (Institute for Energy Research, November 2012), http://tinyurl.com/cm2ra77 (pdf, 13 MB).

emissions. For example, recent improvements in hydraulic fracturing have increased the supply and use of natural gas, which has decreased the total emissions resulting from electricity production.

■ Future generations will probably be wealthier and thus better able to afford to reduce emissions.

■ Forcing cuts in emissions too quickly could require expensive pieces of capital equipment, such as coal-fired electricity generators, to be retired before the end of their useful life.

However, delays also have the potential to increase the cost of reducing emissions, in part because of their effects on technological improvements and decisions about long-lived capital equipment:

■ Taxing carbon later rather than sooner would postpone giving companies an incentive to develop technologies that would lower the cost of reducing CO_2 emissions. Developing new zero- or low-emission technologies, and improving existing ones, would proceed more quickly with a combination of federal support for basic research and development and a steadily rising price on CO_2 emissions.[45]

■ Delays could also lead companies that are replacing long-lived capital equipment today to install new emission-intensive equipment, thus increasing the likelihood that such equipment would have to be retired prematurely in the future if emission-cutting policies went into effect (particularly if the delays caused lawmakers to phase in future emission cuts more rapidly than they might otherwise).

Regardless of the effect that delaying emission reductions might have on the cost of achieving lower emissions, such delays would increase the expected damage from climate change by increasing the risk of very costly, potentially even catastrophic, outcomes. Given the persistent nature of greenhouse gases and the dynamics of climate change, warming would continue for several decades even if emissions were quickly cut to a small fraction of their current levels.[46] In general, the risk of costly damage is higher as the extent of warming increases and as the pace of warming picks up; thus, failing to limit emissions soon increases that risk.

---

45. See Congressional Budget Office, *Evaluating the Role of Prices and R&D in Reducing Carbon Dioxide Emissions* (September 2006), www.cbo.gov/publication/18131.

46. For more information, see Congressional Budget Office, *Potential Impacts of Climate Change in the United States* (May 2009), www.cbo.gov/publication/41180.

About This Document

This Congressional Budget Office (CBO) report was prepared at the request of the Ranking Member of the House Committee on Energy and Commerce. In keeping with CBO's mandate to provide objective, impartial analysis, the report makes no recommendations.

The analysis was prepared by Terry Dinan of CBO's Microeconomic Studies Division with guidance from Joseph Kile. Bruce Arnold, J'nell Blanco, Kim Cawley, Wendy Edelberg, Theresa Gullo, Daniel Hoople, Mark Lasky, Susanne Mehlman, William Randolph (formerly of CBO), Frank Sammartino, Robert Shackleton, Andrew Stocking, Alan van der Hilst, and David Weiner provided helpful comments.

Lawrence Goulder of Stanford University, Chip Knappenberger of the Cato Institute, David Kreutzer of the Heritage Foundation, Gilbert Metcalf of Tufts University, Robert Murphy of the Institute for Energy Research, William Pizer of Duke University, Sebastian Rausch of the Massachusetts Institute of Technology, and Pete Wilcoxen of Syracuse University reviewed the report. The assistance of external reviewers implies no responsibility for the final product, which rests solely with CBO.

Christian Howlett edited the report; Maureen Costantino and Jeanine Rees prepared it for publication; and Maureen Costantino designed the cover. The report is available on CBO's website (www.cbo.gov).

Douglas W. Elmendorf
Director

May 2013

Figure 1.

Return to Reference 1, 2

Effects of a Carbon Tax on Labor, Investment, and Output

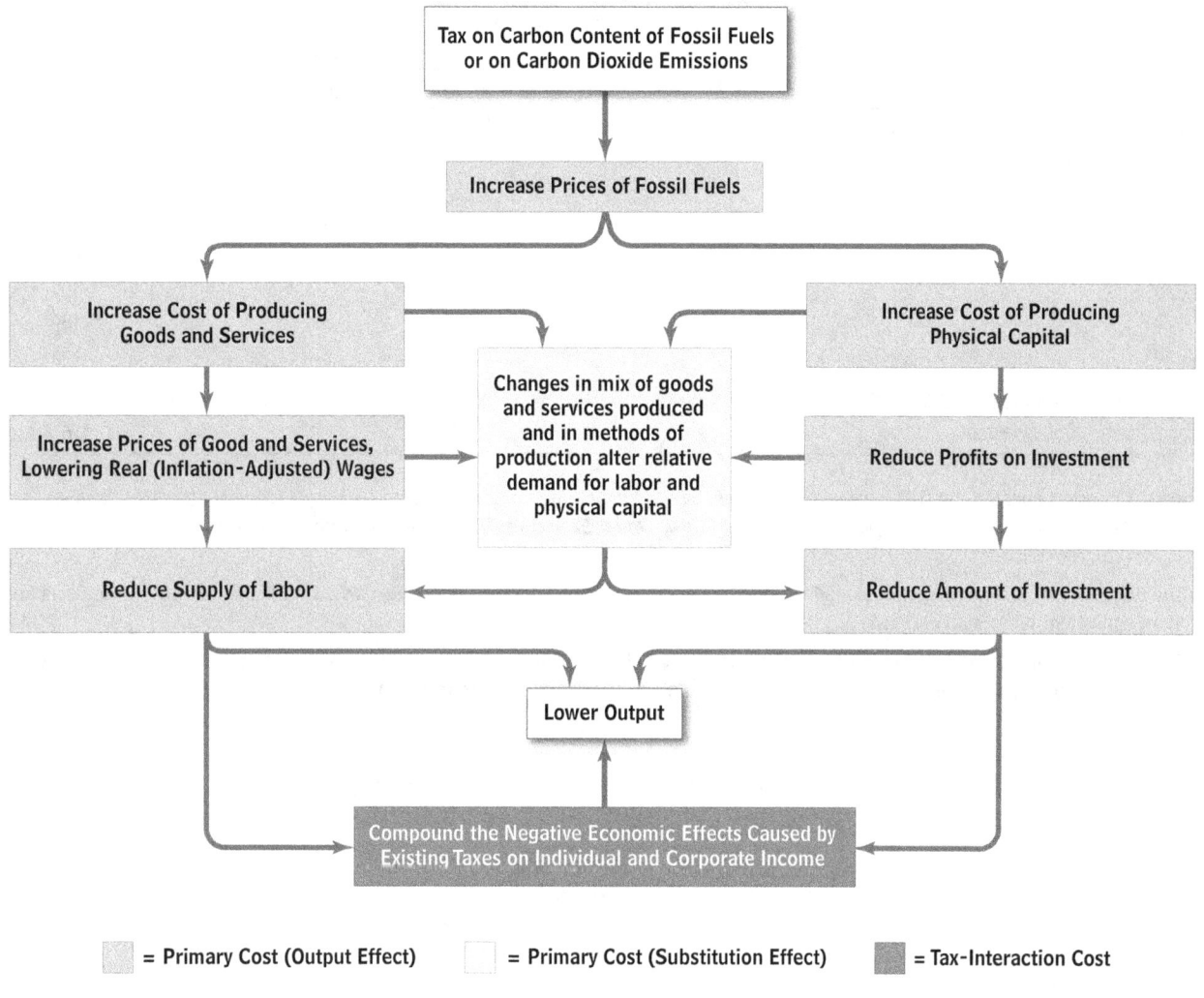

Source: Congressional Budget Office.

Table 1.

Return to Reference 1, 2

The Interagency Working Group's Estimates of the Average Social Cost of Carbon, by Discount Rate

	Discount Rate[a]		
	5 Percent	3 Percent	2.5 Percent
Social Cost of Carbon (Cost per ton of carbon dioxide emissions, in 2007 dollars)[b]			
2010	5	21	35
2015	6	24	38
2020	7	26	42
2030	10	33	50
2040	13	39	58
2050	16	45	65
Average Annual Change in the Social Cost of Carbon, 2010–2050 (Percent)	3.1	1.9	1.6

Source: Congressional Budget Office based on Interagency Working Group on Social Cost of Carbon, *Technical Support Document: Social Cost of Carbon for Regulatory Impact Analysis Under Executive Order 12866* (February 2010), http://go.usa.gov/2une (pdf, 847 KB).

a. The discount rate is the interest rate used to compute a single number that expresses the present value of a flow of future costs in terms of an equivalent lump-sum cost today.

b. Each of these numbers is an average of 15 estimates produced by applying five scenarios with different projections of global economic output, population, and emissions to three different models of the climate and the economy.

www.ingramcontent.com/pod-product-compliance
Lightning Source LLC
Chambersburg PA
CBHW080751290526
45790CB00008B/3403